ONLY

Caroline Natzler

Published by Grenadine Press, 2015
email: grenadinepress@live.co.uk

ISBN: 978-0-9532537-1-5

Acknowledgments; Thanks to the editors of the
following poetry journals in which some of these
poems first appeared; Acumen, Artemis, Envoi,
Iota and Poetry Salzburg Review.
Thanks also to artist Moira Coupe.

British Library Cataloguing in Publication Data.
A CIP record for this book is available from the
British Library.

Cover image by Electric Reads. Rain drop image
supplied by Westa © 123RF.com

Printed by Catford Print Centre

Design by Electric Reads
www.electricreads.com

Contents

To Cathy

For a lifetime of inspirational friendship

Whole

You write about nothing only
and eternity

your touch on the paper colourless as rain

falling

deep into the earth of this dazzling
particular world.

Coming Down

Coming down from the turbulent light
the sun's weight and the far red shift
that shows like a wake the stars' departing

almost numb now to the long ache
do we matter, as we feel, or are we nothing?

losing the urge as you grow old
to strain towards a cosmic whole

left only with odd bits of sadness
like threads hanging loose from the heart

you watch now, from the containing dark of your body
through remnants of blue peeled from the sky

for small stories only

birds flicked into being, flying away, always away
but making such a noise as they go.

Reach

I have had the same hands all this time

have analysed and constructed
in the agitated corners of cities

have dreamed.

What is it I have tried to grasp
all these years?

I become more and more of a thing
as my fingers seize up in the damp.

I still compel each moment
I am.

Extend

You hide from the sky here where it all began,
live in sharp shadows and busyness.

The sheer blue unnerves.

You long for it to form, shuffle into clouds
patchy, comfortable shapes you half recognise

but the only movement here is on the earth,
people labouring against bright emptiness.

You want to find or make something of yours
when you gaze up, away

here where it all began.

Unearth

You root about for the glint of buried words
- oh! squashy when you try them on your teeth

while years behind you
the forest like a grandfather clears its throat

at the outermost
where the foxes say goodnight to each other.

Release

Yet we are jointed into the world
a part of its weight

always something touching

write against the assault of experience
lift it out of the brute minute-to-minute

as if the words could reach
a finer place and redeem

though it's only people who read
- people on their own hard ground

it's only something said
across a neighbour's fence.

Call

You could never hear it -
only the echo

guilt, defining each moment -
that you'd erred

from some lifting way
to faith again, the grace of God
where you should be -
all else sick and grey.

Then death hit, hard by -
clear-cut, factual.
Stopped the echo

left you animal full for your days of life
on open land.

How Else

Not a striving or reaching or clarion mission
but small

it lights on the underside of things

and touched by a breath of intent
- air flickering olive leaves to silver -
or what seems like intent

it says, *beauty*

this small faith

and wants to say
how else but from goodness?

Older

It's not quite god
pocketed deep inside you now

this wording of your inner voice
no longer needing an answer

this chest-centred warmth

stillness of snow
sheltering every branch and twig

not god, only a sense
that this is enough.

Tissue

Never sheer

just this chance and wander

presence breaking sea-light
in the empty room

happening to be

clinking of masts and crunch of shells
fish and chips under the stars

essential bone
and medication to slow its decay

brittle and galactic.

Trying

There is only facing the sun
stumbling on in the blur of the after-image

only seeing how the world is made small by the sky
and opening to some of all that is beyond the sky

the space and the blazing

then turning home to criss-crossed shadows
peculiar hearts.

Art

In each cool marble moment
pupates the next -
hot, and briefly shadowless.

Way Out

You turn from the window in the night

the glaring square that looms too large
or shrinks to the bottom of the dark.

It will never open.

Each breath heaves against your chains,
locks them tighter.

You've heard that time simply happens.

With milder breath
and the patience of a silkworm

you cast around your chains
a mist of pale tissue

soft as down on skin

leaving within each hazed link
a space for vision.

After Liang Shaoji

Inner

I wear my hair loose, grey
soft about my face like an animal

the slight jewels of the dead
glistening on my wrist
fierce pomegranate seeds.

There is a possibility here of touch.

Passing Through

Still open to the wide going of the future
reaching into the day as if to touch the centre

though you mine the night's dreams
not for understanding now

but the instant's vivid charge
without history or consequence

not knowing where you'll be when you wake.

Cycle

Raggle-taggle of flesh and mind
weary of always plotting
for each next moment to come right

you long for stillness, the one
word beyond narrative, to resolve

the shiftiness of time
nudging on night after night
and the always going down of things

until, as if by birdsong rattling in the dark
you are roused, sense how the scramble of words
and the opening of moment into moment

bring abundance, a curious, dappled living

and the sun rising like a story.

Ringing the Changes

Spirits whistling
high on the tricky radiance of happening

glitches and mutations
complexity that grows and falls away

oscillation of invisible strings
vibrations that make all matter

    the music of the spheres

and the bump in data
deep in an underground chamber

the god particle
that gave substance to the universe

your spirits spinning in the infinite regress
of the final secret.

In Time

The failure of all that contriving
to craft a shapely life

may I learn to let it go

we make of our lives profusion, not order

and our partly scorched gold-ish tatters
are not twisted into a neat garland
or wound tight around our bodies, ready for the earth

but blow and sway, uncertain foliage in the dusk
lush leaves of the day.

At the Margin

I thought it was a flake of ash
on swirling brown waters

I thought it was the light of a person
ghosting the dark sky

I thought of all the poems about it
and the silence.

Also by Caroline Natzler

Fiction

Water Wings
Onlywomen Press, 1990

Poetry

Speaking the Wetlands
Pikestaff Press, 1998

Design Fault
Flambard Press, 2001

Smart Dust
Grenadine Press, 2009

Fold
Hearing Eye, 2014